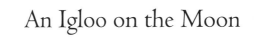

An Igloo on the Moon

For Iris

An Igloo on the Moon

Exploring Architecture

Adrian Buckley and David Jenkins

CIRCA

Simple Forms of Shelter

Human beings are instinctive builders. We have been building for at least 400,000 years. The earliest structures were simple shelters — places to sleep at night or escape from the rain. They would have been shaped from natural materials, gathered locally. If people settled near a forest, they built from wood. In arid climates they might build from mud

bricks, which they would bake in the sun.
In frozen regions they used blocks of snow.
Nomadic peoples devised temporary shelters,
made from fabric or animal skins, which they
could take down and carry from place to place.
More settled societies developed construction
techniques that led to distinctive regional
forms – from igloos to *iQukwane*.

Igloos

In the Arctic, the Inuit people cut blocks of compacted snow to create igloos. A family-sized igloo – or *iglu* in Inuit language – can be constructed very quickly: a skilled team can complete one in as little as an hour. The snow blocks are laid in a spiral, whose radius reduces as it rises. The completed dome is very strong – capable of supporting the weight of a grown man. Animal skins are used to seal the doorway and sheets of ice are sometimes inserted to create windows. Snow is an excellent building material in such a cold climate because the tiny pockets of air trapped within it make it a good insulator, which helps to keep the igloo warm inside.

Arctic region (c.10,000BC to present)

Log cabins

The log cabin originated in the Bronze Age, when coniferous forests covered much of Europe and Scandinavia. The typical cabin is a single-room hut with a door and one or more small windows. Its walls are built from round or hewn logs, laid in horizontal courses. The logs overlap at the corners and are notched to create a rigid structure. The pitched roof can be formed from boards or logs, and the gaps sealed with mud or moss to make the cabin weathertight. In the seventeenth century, Swedish settlers introduced the log cabin to North America, where it became the archetypal home of the American frontiersman.

Northern Europe and North America (c.3500BC to early 20th century)

iQukwane

In Southern Africa, the Zulu people build beehive huts, known as *iQukwane*. The men and women of the village work together to construct them, each applying different skills. The men embed saplings in the ground and bend them to form a beehive frame, using a tree trunk as a central support. The women then clad the frame with thatch, which is held in place with a web of braided reeds. This thick layer of thatch helps to keep the temperature in the hut relatively stable. The floor and the central hearth are made from a mix of animal dung and soil from termite mounds – a material that dries as hard as stone and can be polished smooth.

Southern Africa (c.16th to 20th century)

Adobe houses

Adobe is a building technique ideally suited to arid climates, where its dense walls provide insulation against hot days and cold nights. Adobe bricks are made from a mixture of sand and wet clay, with a binding of straw or animal dung, and cured in the open air. Roofs can be flat or vaulted and domes can be formed. To protect against rain, the brick structure is finished with a layer of render that has to be renewed every year. Adobe originated in ancient Egypt and spread through the Arab world, via the Mediterranean, to Spain and the Americas. These adobe beehive houses, in Harran, Turkey, follow a pattern thought to have existed for more than 3,000 years.

Harran, Turkey (c.1000BC to early 20th century)

Tepees

The Native American people of the Great Plains devised a portable shelter, which they called a *thípi* or 'tepee'. Conical in form, tepees are traditionally made from buffalo skins wrapped around a supporting frame of pine or cedar saplings. The poles are bound together at the apex and the skin is secured at the base with pegs. To allow a fire to be lit inside for heating and cooking, the tepee has an opening at the top, which expels smoke and draws in fresh air. To keep out the rain this opening can be closed off with flaps and a lining of hides or blankets added to make the tepee warmer in winter.

Great Plains, USA (c.11,500BC to early 20th century)

Yurts

The Mongolian yurt — or *ger* — is a portable dwelling,
traditionally used by the nomadic peoples of the
steppes of Central Asia. Like the tepee, a yurt has
a wooden frame covered with a weatherproof skin —
usually a combination of canvas and thick felt made
from lamb's wool. The frame comprises a circular
crown, supported on poles, with radial purlins that
attach to a lattice wall, all tied together with ropes or
ribbons. The lattice is collapsible and folds down into
a compact bundle. A yurt can be erected in as little as
two hours and then dismantled and moved from place
to place on the back of a camel or yak.

Mongolia (c.1000BC to early 20th century)

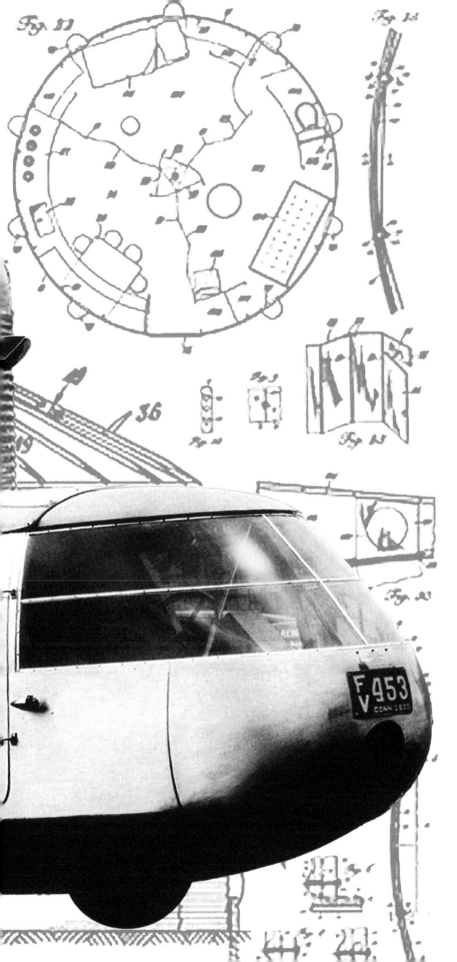

Dymaxion Deployment Unit

Not all simple forms of shelter are hundreds of years old. The Dymaxion Deployment Unit was developed in the mid-twentieth century as a prototype for emergency housing. Circular in plan, with a conical roof – not unlike the American grain silos that inspired its design – it is made from corrugated steel panels, using technology originally developed by the aircraft industry. The house has porthole windows and a rooftop air vent to encourage natural ventilation. Units were to be mass-produced in factories and delivered to site in kit form. Cheap, lightweight and demountable, it is the modern equivalent of the yurt.

USA (1940) Designer: Richard Buckminster Fuller

Keeping Cool and Staying Warm

Depending on where you are in the world, and the season, controlling comfort can mean very different things. Beneath the harsh desert sun, you need to find shade. In the tropics, where the air is still and heavy with moisture, you crave a cooling breeze. In the depths of a North American winter, you want to stay warm. Long before central heating and

mechanical air conditioning were invented,
people employed a variety of traditional
methods to control the climate in the spaces
they inhabited, whether inside or outside.
Instead of technology they relied on ingenuity,
using ancient techniques that were energy
efficient and environmentally sustainable
– from pools of water to windcatchers.

The *impluvium*

Ancient Greek and Roman houses enjoyed a natural form of air conditioning, which used a process known as 'evaporative cooling'. The living spaces in these houses were arranged around an atrium, which was open to the sky. In the middle of the atrium was an *impluvium* – a sunken area designed to collect rainwater. From the *impluvium*, water drained into an underground cistern, where it was stored. In the heat of the summer this water would be drawn up and poured back into the impluvium. As the water warmed, it evaporated, so cooling the surrounding air. Cool air is heavier than warm air and so a current was created in which fresh air was drawn down into the atrium, chilled and dispersed throughout the house.

Greece, Asia Minor and Italy (c.600BC to 400AD)

Shōji screens

A traditional Japanese house has one large living space, or *ima*, which is subdivided by sliding partitions. The floor of the *ima* is covered with *tatami* mats and any part of the space can be used for living or sleeping. Translucent screens, or *shōji*, made from wood and paper, line the perimeter of the house. The *shōji* can slide back in warm weather to connect the house with nature – a relationship that is symbolically important in Japanese culture. In the summer months, when the climate is hot and humid, the open screens encourage cross ventilation through the house. Projecting roofs protect the *shōji* from the rain and shade the house from the high summer sun. At night, and in the typhoon season, the house is sealed with wooden shutters.

Japan (c.16th to late 19th century)

Windcatchers

A windcatcher is a device used in hot, arid climates to create natural ventilation in a building. Windcatchers originated in ancient Persia and are found throughout the Middle East, where they are known as *bâdgirs*. Yazd, in Iran, is a 'city of *bâdgirs*'. Its buildings are constructed from adobe, with dense walls to absorb the fierce summer heat. Raised above the rooftops are tall, chimney-like structures, which are oriented to catch the prevailing wind. Warm air drawn into a *bâdgir* takes on moisture and cools; and as it does so it sinks. By the time it is released at the bottom of the duct, it feels refreshingly chilled. It is a desert air-conditioning system driven by nothing more than solar power.

Yazd, Iran (c.AD100 to 19th century)

Verandas

Verandas are a feature of many colonial-era buildings around the world, from Australian vernacular dwellings to South African homesteads and Indian bungalows. The veranda is a very effective way of creating shade and establishing a buffer zone between inside and outside. Colonial settlers developed distinctive architectural styles in which traditional European building types were adapted to suit the realities of hot, sometimes subtropical climates. Deep verandas are supported by slender pillars or delicate cast-iron tracery. Some of these verandas are large enough to be used as external rooms – places to sit during the heat of the day or to sleep at night.

Australia (c.1850–1900)

Brise-soleil

A brise-soleil is a fixed sunscreen. In regions where the summer sun is particularly fierce, a brise-soleil is sometimes used to deflect the sun's rays and provide natural shade. This office tower was designed for the Ministry of Education and Health in Rio de Janeiro and was one of the first modern buildings to incorporate a brise-soleil. The brise-soleil takes the form of slender horizontal and vertical concrete 'blades'. The blades are positioned so that they block the high summer sun, which would otherwise cause the building to overheat. In the winter, in contrast, when the sun is at its lowest, the brise-soleil allows sunlight to penetrate the glazing and have a gentle warming effect.

Rio de Janeiro, Brazil (1937-43)

Architect: Lucio Costa with Oscar Niemeyer and others

Canopies

Fabric canopies have been used for centuries to provide protection from the sun. In ancient Rome, a retractable sailcloth awning – called a *velarium* – was used to shade spectators in the Colosseum. Parasols and umbrellas perform a similar function. The umbrellas illustrated here are on a gigantic scale. They were designed for the piazza of the Prophet's Mosque in Medina – a destination for hundreds of thousands of pilgrims after the Hajj to Mecca. Without shade, during the heat of the day the piazza would be inhospitable. The umbrellas have folding arms, which open as the sun rises. As the arms spread out, the fabric membrane is stretched taut and the square becomes a shaded oasis.

Medina, Saudi Arabia (1992-2011) Architect: Bodo Rasch

The hearth

Lighting a fire is the oldest way of keeping warm. The hearth was often located centrally at the heart of a house or a great hall, where people would gather to enjoy the comfort it provided. The American architect Frank Lloyd Wright, who created some of the greatest houses of the last century, believed that the hearth was 'the psychological centre of the home.' He used the hearth to provide a social focus as well as a source of warmth. This house – called 'Fallingwater' – sits above a fast-flowing waterfall in rural Pennsylvania. The fireplace in the living room is placed symbolically on the exposed bedrock, where a campfire might once have been set, to emphasise the house's connection with nature.

Bear Run, Pennsylvania, USA (1935-39) Architect: Frank Lloyd Wright

Exploring New Types of Structure

Over time, as societies grew technologically more sophisticated, they explored new ways of building. That in turn led to the invention of new structural forms. The ancient Greeks honed and perfected post-and-beam construction, turning it into an artistic discipline. The Romans introduced concrete, which allowed them to construct domes on an epic scale. Medieval Japanese craftsmen built ingeniously in timber – a tradition that lives on. Nineteenth-century foundry masters pioneered lightweight structures wrought from iron and glass. Modern architects and engineers are able to experiment with structural form in entirely novel ways – from Sydney Opera House to the Centre Pompidou.

The primitive hut

For centuries, historians have speculated about the
beginnings of architecture. Some have suggested that
the earliest buildings were wooden structures – not
built from cut logs and planks, but shaped from the
living trunks and branches. Or perhaps posts were
planted upright in the ground and horizontal members
fixed to them to form beams, with a roof added, to
shed rainwater? Japanese archaeologists have discovered
traces of what may be the world's oldest huts, on
a hillside north of Tokyo. Wooden posts found
embedded in the earth have been dated to 500,000
years ago. The imaginary structure pictured here is the
so-called 'primitive hut'. This is how historians once
thought the first rustic cabins might have looked.

Illustration after Abbé Marc-Antoine Laugier (1755)

The Parthenon

In ancient Greek culture, mathematics, art and architecture were intertwined. The Greeks devised a Classical system, known as 'orders', which governed the proportions of a building, down to the smallest detail. There were three Greek orders – the Doric, Ionic and Corinthian – which were progressively more ornate. The design of a Doric-order building, such as The Parthenon, therefore followed a predetermined pattern. While it is structurally very simple – stone lintels span between columns to create an entablature, on which rests a pitched roof – sculpturally it is very sophisticated. Every surface is shaped and moulded, from the fluting on the columns to the figures in the pediment.

Athens, Greece (477-438BC) Architects: Ictinus and Callicrates

The Pantheon

In ancient Greece, architects were concerned with
perfection. In ancient Rome they were driven by
invention. Like the Parthenon, the Pantheon was
originally a temple, but there all similarities end. It is
among the most daring of all Roman buildings, not
least for its dome, which is still the largest unreinforced
concrete structure in the world. Internally, the dome
measures 150 Roman feet (43.3 metres) in diameter.
To reach that incredible size and not collapse under
its own weight, the dome had to be cleverly engineered.
Its structure reduces in thickness from the base to the
top, and concealed chambers within the shell form
a honeycomb to combine lightness with strength.

Rome, Italy (c.AD126) Architect: Apollodorus of Damascus

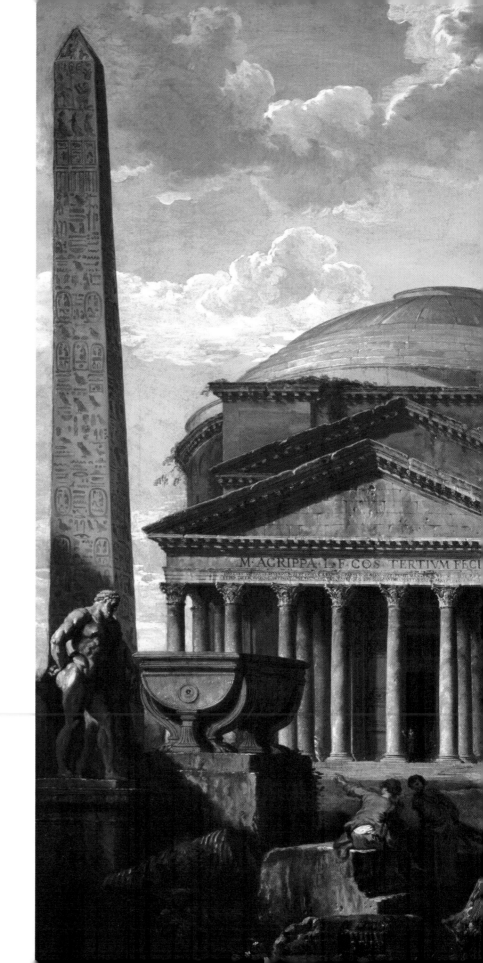

Chartres Cathedral

Chartres is perhaps the finest French Gothic cathedral.
Go inside and the stonework appears incredibly
delicate and the nave soars almost impossibly high.
The brilliant structural innovation that makes this
spatial drama possible is the flying buttress – the
'secret ingredient' of all the great Gothic cathedrals.
The buttresses flank the nave and choir to brace
against the lateral forces of the ceiling vault, which
means that the walls no longer have to perform that
role. So instead of being massive, the walls can be
tall and slender and the windows enlarged to become
luminescent planes of glass. Instead of gloom,
all is space and light.

Chartres, France (1020-1260)

Great Mosque of Djenné

How big a structure can you create from mud?
The answer is to be found in Africa and the Great
Mosque of Djenné, which is the most magnificent
mud-brick building in the world. The walls of the
mosque are made from blocks of sun-baked earth,
called *ferey*, which are bonded with sand-and-earth-
based mortar. A smooth layer of plaster inside and
out gives the building a moulded appearance – as
if it were formed in one piece. Pipes project from
the roof to prevent rainwater from washing away
the plasterwork, and bundles of palm sticks – called
toron – are embedded in the walls at regular intervals.
The toron serve as scaffolding for repairs to the
plaster, which must be carried out every year.

Djenné, Mali (13th century; rebuilt in 1907)

Ise Shrine

The Ise Shrine (*Ise Jingū*) is an example of how the essence of a 'perfect' structure can be preserved, even as the fabric itself decays and rots away. The wooden temple buildings at Ise are at once both ancient and modern. For although they were designed centuries ago, their fabric is replaced in a twenty-year cycle, in accordance with the Shinto belief in death and rebirth and the impermanence of all things (*wabi-sabi*). Each renewal takes eight years to complete and requires more than 12,000 cypress logs – some more than 200 years old. Culturally, rebuilding is a way of ensuring that craft skills are maintained and handed down from one generation to the next.

Ise City, Japan (c.4BC–present; last rebuilt in 2013)

The Crystal Palace

Picture a structure as large as a cathedral, but as delicate and transparent as a glass bowl – that's how the Crystal Palace must have appeared to visitors in 1851. It was breathtaking, dazzling and new. Nothing like it had been seen before on this scale. Erected in Hyde Park as a venue for The Great Exhibition, it provided a showcase for the products of art and industry from around the world. The design of the building was determined by the dimensions of the most common component – the panes of glass, which measured 25cm wide by 125cm long, the largest available at that time. Designed in just two weeks, the Crystal Palace was completed in less than a year. When the exhibition closed, it was dismantled, piece-by-piece, and re-erected on a new site in South London.

London, England (1851; destroyed 1936) Architect: Sir Joseph Paxton

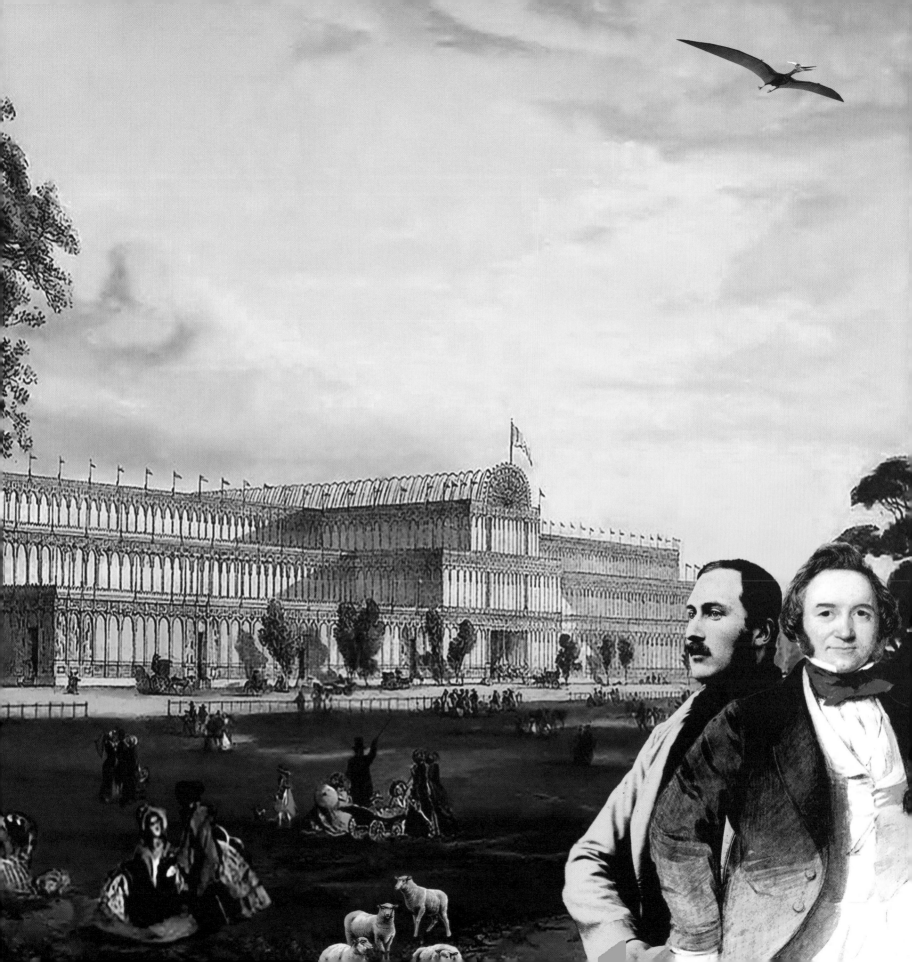

Sydney Opera House

Sydney Opera House is among the world's most recognisable and iconic structures. The architect modelled the building's distinctive roofs as 'shells' — made as if cutting pieces from an orange peel and placing them together. They would have been the largest reinforced-concrete shell structures ever attempted. However, the engineers could not find a way of constructing them economically and so the shells are formed using a system of precast-concrete panels supported on ribs with a spherical geometry. From a distance, the shells appear perfectly smooth and uniformly white, but their 'sparkle' is an optical effect, the result of more than a million tiles with two different glazes — matte cream and gloss white.

Sydney, Australia (1957-73) Architect: Jørn Utzon

Centre Georges Pompidou

What would we look like if our bones, arteries and organs were draped around the outside of our bodies, instead of beneath the skin? We might look like the Centre Pompidou, which structurally is inside out. The beams and columns, the escalators, ductwork and piping, and all the other installations you would normally expect to find concealed inside are instead displayed around the perimeter, where they become in effect the architecture. As a museum it is revolutionary. Instead of being closed and forbidding, it is open and welcoming. In place of galleries, it has flexible exhibition floors. As a building it is shocking. Critics once derided it as a 'monster'. Yet it is one of the most popular cultural destinations in the world.

Paris, France (1971-77) Architects: Piano and Rogers

Living Beneath the Ground

The earliest known European cave paintings can be found on Spain's Cantabrian Sea coast. They are 40,000 years old and are evidence that humans still chose to inhabit caves long after they had developed the tools and techniques to create structures of their own. Even in some advanced societies it was considered more appropriate to burrow down rather than build.

Entire buildings might be carved into the living rock face or networks of catacombs excavated far below ground. Sometimes whole communities were constructed that way. In modern times, engineers tunnel beneath cities to create underground transport networks and architects dig down to ensure that new buildings are visually discreet.

Rock-cut dwellings

The contours of the Göreme Valley, in central Turkey, were shaped over millennia by wind and water, which ate away at the volcanic tufo to leave a skyline of spiky peaks and rocky outcrops. However, it is what came next that makes this landscape special. As people settled here, they discovered that the rock was soft and easy to cut and so they bored straight into it to create dwellings. The result is an incredible cave world, with houses, stables, workshops and places of worship all carved into the rock. In some places the tunnel complexes are so extensive that they would once have functioned virtually as 'cities' far below ground.

Cappadocia, Turkey (c.1800BC onwards)

Petra

Petra stands on what was once a major trading route — a caravan crossroads between Arabia, Egypt and Syria-Phoenicia. It is surrounded by mountains and approached via a narrow natural cleft — the Siq — which threads its way for a mile between sheer rock walls. At the head of the Siq stands the Treasury, or *Al Khazneh*. The Treasury's sunlit facade is the first glimpse visitors have of the city as they emerge from the gloom. It was constructed as a mausoleum at the beginning of the first century AD and like many of Petra's buildings — which span ancient Eastern, Hellenistic and Roman traditions — it is entirely monolithic, carved directly into the red sandstone from which Petra takes its popular name: the 'Rose City'.

Petra, Jordan (2nd century BC to 2nd century AD)

Catacombs

Imagine a society in which religion is suppressed and it is illegal to bury the dead. Ancient Rome was once such a place. Jews and Christians believed in burial, but Roman law demanded cremation. The solution was the catacombs, where Jewish and Christian families could lay their relatives to rest. Catacombs were excavated outside Roman jurisdiction, along the main roads into the city. Over time, vast networks of passageways, or *ambulacra*, were carved from the volcanic tufo. Bodies were sealed in coffins, or sarcophagi, which were interred in niches or set within recesses. The larger chambers were decorated with frescoes and some were dedicated as chapels.

Rome, Italy (2nd to 5th centuries)

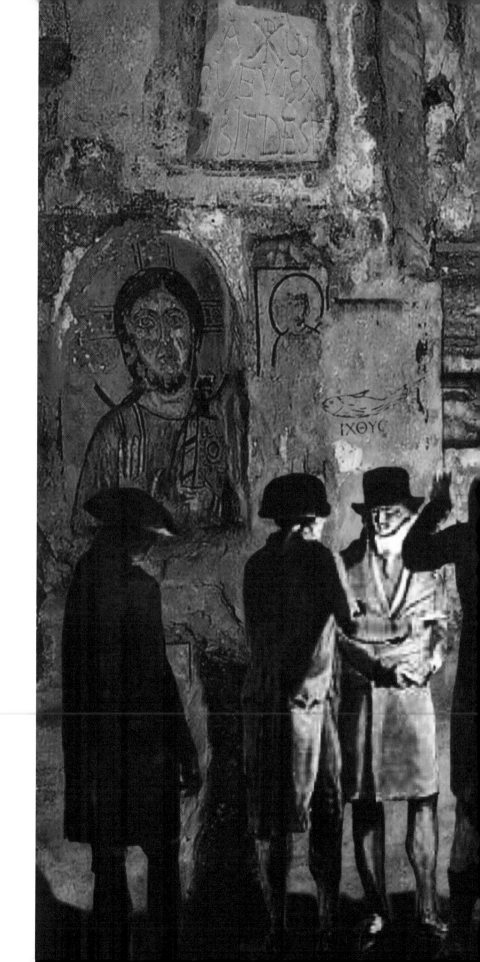

Yaodongs

In the Loess Plateau of northern China, many millions of people live in house-caves, or yaodongs. Their development appears to stand conventional wisdom on its head, with dwellings below ground and fields and roads above, but in a region where building materials are scarce they offer an ideal solution. Loess is silt, which is soft and easy to work. Yaodongs are typically arranged around open courtyards, with the houses cut directly into the earth. The rooms have vaulted ceilings to give structural strength. They open into the courtyards and back on to the loess, which provides thermal insulation, helping to keep the houses cool in summer and warm in winter.

Loess Plateau, China (2000BC–AD1900)

Stepwells

Stepwells originated in the arid states of India – such as Gujarat and Rajasthan – where they provided communities with a year-round source of fresh water. Many survive intact, but unused. The finest examples fall somewhere between engineering and art – virtual palaces underground – with elaborate sculptural schemes whose treatment varies according to Hindu or Muslim tradition. The well itself was usually far below ground, accessed via a long stair, or stairs, set within a stone-lined cutting. In the monsoon season the cutting became a cistern for rainwater storage. The most magnificent stepwells are organised into several tiers and some incorporate canopies to provide shade for the women, whose role it was to collect the water.

Chand Baori Stepwell, Jaipur, India (9th century)

Churches of Lalibela

Lalibela, in Ethiopia, has been a place of pilgrimage
for Coptic Christians since the twelfth century.
It is famous for its eleven sunken churches, which are
located within a network of subterranean courtyards
and passages. The churches are attributed to King
Lalibela, who sought to create a 'New Jerusalem' in
Ethiopia after Muslim conquests halted Christian
pilgrimages to the Holy Land. Each of the churches
is sculpted from the living rock – a process that would
have involved boring through the volcanic stone to
create a rough geometric form before the masons could
begin the work of carving window and door openings,
architraves and other fine details. Why they were built
that way remains a mystery.

Lalibela, Ethiopia (c.12th to 13th century)

Metro Stations

Many cities have underground rail systems. London has the oldest, Moscow probably the most extravagant and Tokyo certainly the busiest. Stockholm's metro is a relative latecomer, begun only in the 1940s, but it is remarkable for the radical design of its stations and the way in which they are decorated. It has been described as the 'longest art gallery in the world'. Many of the station caverns were cut directly into the bedrock. The rough rock face has been left exposed and celebrated as a reminder of the fact that travellers are circulating deep below ground. The caverns are painted in vivid colours to create an atmospheric underworld for Stockholm's commuters.

Stockholm, Sweden (1941-present) Architects: Peter Celsing and others

Underground house

Sometimes there are environmental reasons for building underground. This house lies in the Pembrokeshire Coast National Park – an unspoiled landscape in which permission to build is rarely granted. The solution in this case was camouflage. The house is so successfully dug into its clifftop site that from most viewpoints it is effectively invisible. From a distance it appears as a grassy hillock. Only where it faces the sea does it open up to capture the view, its glazed wall looking out like a beady eye. The turf roof provides very effective thermal insulation and so helps to moderate the temperature within the house throughout the year.

Druidston, Wales (1994-98) Architects: Future Systems

Habitable Bridges and Heroic Spans

Is a bridge a work of architecture or a feat of engineering? The answer is often 'both'. Bridges can take an almost infinite variety of forms, from simple decks to habitable structures, from ropes slung between piers to monumental viaducts. The Romans built spectacularly in stone, and with incredible accuracy. The Incas built quickly and deftly using rope. With the Industrial Revolution in the nineteenth century came new materials – iron and steel – and ever-greater structural daring. Alongside their value as physical connections, bridges also have a symbolic role. Just as a skyscraper can become an icon for its city or region, so can a bridge – from the Pont du Gard to the Millau Viaduct.

The Pont du Gard

The Pont du Gard once formed part of a Roman aqueduct that brought water to the inhabitants of Nemausus (Nîmes), in southern France. It is the most ambitious structure of its type ever conceived. Three arched tiers carry a water conduit — or *specus* — 49 metres above the River Gardon. The Romans built in stone, with incredible precision. The aqueduct stretched over 50 kilometres from a spring at Uzès and the *specus* fell at a gradient of 1 in 3,000 — a fall so gentle that it is imperceptible to the human eye. At its peak, the aqueduct brought 200 million litres of water daily into Nîmes, where it was piped to the city's fountains, public baths and private homes.

Gorges du Gardon, France (1st century AD)

Inca rope bridge

The Incas were the most sophisticated builders in pre-Columbian America. Within the Inca Empire was a road network that extended some 40,000 kilometres and crossed rivers and mountain gorges. As the Incas had no wheeled transport – traffic comprised people and livestock – bridges were lightweight, made from rope and wood. Q'eswachaka, in Peru, has the last surviving example of an Inca suspension bridge. It spans 28 metres between massive stone piers. Its cables are hand woven, using long grasses and other organic fibres, and the deck is reinforced with battens. Although rope is very strong, it decays over time and so the cables are renewed annually, following ancient tradition.

Huinchiri, Peru (15th century to present)

Old London Bridge

It might seem novel today, but it was once common in European cities for bridges to be lined with shops and houses. Some were even communities in their own right. By far the longest and most sophisticated of these habitable bridges was Old London Bridge, which spanned the Thames between the City of London and Southwark. Plots on the deck were originally sold to help finance the bridge's construction. By the sixteenth century the bridge supported 200 buildings, some of them magnificent. The bridge was narrow by modern standards – only 8 metres wide – and the roadway was rendered a dark canyon, shared by carts, cattle, coaches and pedestrians. The bridge was often so congested that it could take an hour to cross.

London, England (built 1176-1209; demolished 1831)

Rialto Bridge

For almost three hundred years, the only way to cross the Grand Canal on foot was to use the Rialto Bridge. It is the oldest bridge across the canal and one of the outstanding architectural and engineering achievements of the Italian Renaissance. When it was proposed, its shallow-arch structure was regarded as so audacious that some predicted its collapse. A single stone arch – high enough to allow galleys to pass – supports a broad deck that carries two rows of kiosks. There are three stepped pathways – two along the outer balustrades and a wider central route. The Rialto district is the mercantile heart of Venice, and so it seems natural that the bridge itself should be packed with traders.

Venice, Italy (1588-91) Architect: Antonio da Ponte

The Iron Bridge

The Industrial Revolution introduced materials that transformed the way architects and engineers thought about structure. The Iron Bridge was a product of that revolution – the first to be built from cast iron. Cast iron is weak in tension, but strong in compression. The bridge therefore has an arch form, in which all the structural members are in compression. Cast iron was so untried that there was no 'language' for its assembly and so the foundry adapted woodworking joints – mortise and tenon, dovetails and wedges. The bridge crossed the River Severn in a region where industry was about to boom. So great was its economic impact that an entire town sprang up around it.

Coalbrookdale, England (1777-81) Architect: Thomas Farnolls Pritchard

Garabit Viaduct

The Iron Bridge and the Garabit Viaduct were completed 100 years apart. They represent a century of progress. One is built from cast iron, the other from wrought iron. One spans 30 metres; the longest span of the other is 165 metres. Wrought iron is malleable and strong in tension. It is so superior to cast iron that its introduction allowed huge structural advances. The Garabit Viaduct was once the highest railway bridge in the world, soaring 124 metres above the River Truyère. To minimise weight and improve resistance to wind forces, the bridge's designer, Gustave Eiffel, used a system of open trusses – a solution he would use again in the construction of his Paris tower.

Ruynes-en-Margeride, France (1882-85) Engineer: Gustave Eiffel

Brooklyn Bridge

The Brooklyn Bridge is remarkable in many respects. It was the first steel-cable suspension bridge in the world, with the longest span – 486 metres from tower to tower – and when it was completed its towers were the tallest structures in the Western hemisphere. It was an expression in granite and steel of New York's energy and dynamism. The bridge originally carried trains, trams, cars, bicycles and pedestrians on segregated decks – virtually an entire city on the move. Because the technology used in the bridge's construction was untried, its designers determined that the structure should be six times stronger than necessary. They added a secondary array of cables, which give the bridge its web-like appearance.

New York, USA (1869-83) Engineers: John Augustus Roebling and Washington Roebling

Millau Viaduct

A century on from the Brooklyn Bridge, engineers
have a new set of materials at their disposal –
reinforced concrete and high-tensile steel. They also
have digital technologies that allow them to design
to very fine tolerances. The Millau Viaduct is one
of the highest bridges in the world, in one of Europe's
most magnificent natural settings. It is 2.46 kilometres
long and its highest pier is taller than the Eiffel
Tower. Yet its design is so delicately balanced, and so
structurally poised, that it seems to fit the landscape
perfectly. It is a cable-stayed structure, in which cables
fan out from masts to support the road deck. The
architect decided to paint the cables white, so that
they recede when seen against the sky.

Millau, France (1996-2004) Architect: Foster + Partners;
Engineer: Michel Virlogeux

Reaching up to the Sky

In the ancient world, the tallest structures were monuments such as tombs or victory columns. In the Middle Ages, the highest peaks on city skylines would have been cathedral spires or the minarets of mosques. Until the mid-nineteenth century, when ascending from floor to floor meant climbing a staircase, habitable buildings rarely exceeded ten storeys. The invention of the Otis Elevator in 1852 and the advent of the structural steel frame changed all that forever. Suddenly a tower could be as tall as funds or a city's authorities would allow. A century later 'skyscrapers' were commonplace. Today a new generation of 'megatall' towers of 100 storeys or more dominate horizons around the globe.

Tower of Babel

From the dawn of civilisation, people have dreamt
of building towers tall enough to touch the sky.
The Tower of Babel is the most famous of these
fantastic structures. Described in the Old Testament as
'a tower with its top in the heavens', it was constructed
by the united peoples of the Earth in celebration of
their common language. The name Babel may refer
to the ancient city of Babylon, whose ruins are in
modern-day Iraq. It has also been associated with
the Etemenanki – a Babylonian ziggurat. Many artists
have depicted the Tower of Babel, usually as a spiralling
structure with a wide circular base. Some of them
show the tower in a state of partial collapse as if
to emphasise the futility of aiming so high.

Babylon, Iraq (date unknown)

Great Pyramid of Giza

Built as a tomb for the Fourth Dynasty Egyptian pharaoh Khufu, the Great Pyramid of Giza is one of the Seven Wonders of the Ancient World. For nearly 4,000 years it was also the world's tallest structure. The Great Pyramid was originally cased in smooth white limestone, though only the rough stepped core structure survives. Historians disagree about how it was constructed, though we know that it comprises some 2.3 million granite and limestone blocks and is believed to have taken as little as twenty years to complete – a feat that would have required an astonishing 800 tonnes of stonework to be manoeuvred into place every single day.

Giza, Egypt (c.2560BC) Architect: Hemiunu; Height: 146.6 metres

Minaret of Samarra

The Minaret of Samarra – or Malwiya Minaret –
dates from the middle of the ninth century and
possibly inspired the medieval image of the mythical
Tower of Babel. Malwiya translates as 'snail shell'.
The minaret's conical form makes it unique in Islamic
architecture, though its winding ramp may reflect the
influence of the much earlier Mesopotamian ziggurats,
whose ruins can be found in the region. Originally the
minaret was linked by bridge to the Great Mosque of
Samarra, of which only the outer walls survive. The
vestibule at the top of the ramp would once have been
used by the Muezzin for the *adhan*, or call to prayer.

Samarra, Iraq (848-52) Height: 51.5 metres

Towers of Bologna

In the early Middle Ages Bologna was a city of 'skyscrapers' with up to 100 towers — almost like a medieval Manhattan. Little is known about why these brick towers were built or how they were originally used. The city's leading families may have erected them as symbols of wealth and power. Or they may have been constructed for defensive purposes — perhaps as refuges in the event of an attack on the city. Over time most of these slender masonry structures either collapsed under their own weight or were demolished before they could fall. The most famous survivors are the Asinelli and Garisenda towers — the Two Towers — which stand side-by-side in the heart of the city.

Bologna, Italy (1109-19) Asinelli Tower, height: 97.2 metres

and Garisenda Tower, height: 48 metres

ECCLESIÆ CATHEDRALIS
LINCOLNIENSIS
FACIES OCCIDENTALIS.

Lincoln Cathedral

The Gothic cathedral builders strove to create ever-more magnificent structures. Often they were too ambitious and overreached themselves. Towers would fall and vaults collapse. Lincoln's story combines heroic failure with spectacular success. It has three towers, the tallest of which rises above the central crossing. The first crossing tower collapsed under its own weight in 1237. But when it was rebuilt in 1311, with a spire that soared to 160 metres, it overtook the Great Pyramid of Giza to become the tallest structure in the world. The spire was framed in wood to make it structurally light. Unfortunately, in 1549 it blew down in a storm and was never replaced.

Lincoln, England (1088-1311) Height of crossing tower 83 metres; height of original spire 160 metres

La Sagrada Família

The Basilica and Expiatory Church of the Sagrada Família (Holy Family), which has been under construction for more than 100 years, is as much a statement of artistic faith as it is a work of architecture. It can almost be thought of as a gigantic piece of Art Nouveau sculpture, in which every column, facade and surface is carved, shaped or decorated. When the basilica is completed, it will have an unprecedented eighteen spires, representing in ascending order of height the Twelve Apostles, the Virgin Mary, the four Evangelists and in the centre, standing tallest of all, Jesus Christ. Surmounted by a giant cross, the Christ spire will reach 170 metres, making the Sagrada Família the tallest church building in the world.

Barcelona, Spain (1882 to c.2026) Architect: Antoni Gaudí;
completed by others; Height of the central tower: 170 metres

PARTIE SUPÉRIEURE ENSEMBLE ET DÉTAILS.

PARIS

Je t'aime

I love you

VILLE D'AMOUR

88   1888   14 septembre 1   octobre 1888   14 novembre 1888   26 décembre 1888   20 ja   19   12 mars 1889

Eiffel Tower

The Eiffel Tower was one of the most daring structures of the nineteenth century – the tallest wrought-iron structure ever built, the wonder of its age. It was commissioned as the focal point of the 1889 Exposition Universelle and intended as a tribute to French science and industry. When it was first proposed, critics derided it as a 'hateful column of bolted sheet metal', but it quickly became a popular Paris landmark. Hundreds of thousands of people flocked to see it. Hydraulic lifts led visitors to platforms containing restaurants, a theatre and viewing galleries. By 1909, when the time came to take the tower down, it was such a Parisian icon that it was decided to preserve it forever.

Paris, France (1887-89) Engineer: Gustave Eiffel; Height: 324 metres

14 août 1888   14 septembre 1888   14 octobre 1888   14 novembre

Tatlin's Tower

Vladimir Tatlin's Constructivist tower was conceived
in the wake of the Russian Revolution. It was to be the
headquarters of the Third International or Comintern
– the international Communist organisation founded
by Lenin. At 400 metres high, it would easily have
dwarfed the Eiffel Tower. Tatlin configured the tower
as a tapering double helix. The gigantic steel armature
was to contain four geometric blocks, each of which
would have rotated at different speeds. Within these
structures were to be an auditorium, offices, a press
and information centre and a radio transmitter,
beaming Soviet propaganda around the world.
It is another Tower of Babel, this time dedicated
to spreading the word of Bolshevism.

St Petersburg, Russia (1919) Architect: Vladimir Tatlin; Height: 400 metres

Einstein Tower

The Einstein Tower (*Einsteinturm*) is an astrophysical observatory and laboratory. Although it is not physically very tall, it reaches far into the sky in another sense – it was built to allow research into Albert Einstein's theory of relativity. Light from a solar telescope in the dome is directed down through a shaft at the centre of the tower to instruments in the basement laboratory. Although the interior simply functions as a shell to house scientific equipment, the exterior is exuberant – representing a dynamic expression of the mystique of Einstein's universe. When the tower was completed, the architect took Einstein on a tour. The great man said nothing, until hours after the visit, and then summed it up in just one word: 'organic'.

Potsdam, Germany (1919-24) Architect: Erich Mendelsohn;
Height: 20 metres

Empire State Building

In 1900 a skyscraper race began in Manhattan.
For thirty years architects designed ever taller and
more exotic towers, each vying to outshine the other.
For a brief moment the Chrysler Building was the
tallest. And then the Empire State Building came
along. When it opened on May 1st 1931 it was not
just the tallest office building in the world, but also
the most advanced. Among its many innovations were
an observation deck on the 86th floor and a docking
station for airships at its summit. It was remarkable
not only for its height but also for the speed with
which it was constructed. Framed in steel and
assembled virtually on a production line, it was
completed in just 410 days.

New York, USA (1929-31) Architect: Shreve, Lamb and Harmon;
Height: 443 metres

Burj Khalifa

Cities seeking to establish themselves on the global map vie with one another to build the tallest towers. Larger and more ambitious than ever before, these towers provide cities with an instantly recognisable skyline – much as church or cathedral spires did in the Middle Ages. The Burj Khalifa in Dubai is the ultimate in 'megatall' towers, with an elongated spiralling form that refers to the Minaret of Samarra. It is not only the world's tallest structure, it has more storeys than any other building, the highest occupied floor, the highest restaurant, and its lifts have the longest travel distance. Most importantly, it secured Dubai's place at the top of the high-rise chart.

Dubai, United Arab Emirates (2004-10) Architect: SOM;
Height: 829.8 metres

Visions of the Future

At the beginning of the twentieth century,
as cities grew increasingly polluted, dirty and
dangerous, visionary planners and architects
began to imagine new ways of living. Housing
might be placed harmoniously in nature, or
apartment towers integrated in parkland.
The centres of some older cities could be
roofed over and air conditioned, or brand

new cities created, using building blocks
made on factory production lines. Today,
as we face the challenges of global climate
change, the need for sustainable patterns
of development is greater than ever. Before
long, we may be living in 'farmscrapers'
or in floating cities that sail the seas.
We might even build on the Moon.

Broadacre City

If you were raising a family amid the noise and grime of a North American city then you might be drawn by the prospect of a smallholding and the tranquillity of the countryside. Broadacre City envisaged mass-migration from the city to the suburbs. It proposed that every American household be given a one-acre plot, from the federal land reserves, on which they might build a house and grow their own food. New communities would be created, with all the benefits of rural living. The weakness of the plan was that it required people to drive everywhere. Intensive car use brings high levels of air pollution, greenhouse gas emissions and fuel consumption, all of which are damaging in environmental terms.

USA (1932-59) Architect: Frank Lloyd Wright

La Ville Radieuse

Why try to patch up the crumbling districts of historic cities? Far better to knock them down and start again. That was the starting point for this revolutionary proposal. Instead of living clustered around gloomy little courtyards, people were to be raised high in spacious apartment towers, with running tracks and lidos on their roofs, bathed in sunlight and surrounded by greenery. In place of narrow streets there would be parkland. The roar of traffic would be replaced by the sound of birdsong. It might have been a poetic vision, but in the wrong hands it became a blueprint for mile after mile of anonymous housing blocks and social alienation. As an idea it was a heroic failure.

France (1924) Architect: Le Corbusier

Domed cities

Wouldn't cities be wonderful if they were under cover?
They could be warmer in winter, cooler in summer
and you would never need an umbrella. In the 1960s
the idea of a domed city captivated architects. This
proposal for a dome over Manhattan was by far the
most ambitious. A three-kilometer diameter geodesic
dome would have covered Midtown from the East
River to the Hudson, and from 21st to 64th Streets.
Seen from above it would have been a silvery bubble.
From within, it would have been so delicate as to
almost disappear. Geodesic domes are efficient,
lightweight structures. This one was to be fabricated
in segments and installed with the help of a fleet
of Sikorsky helicopters.

New York, USA (1960) Designer: Richard Buckminster Fuller

Habitat 67

Could a city ever be constructed from hundreds of identical units, all made in a factory? The answer is yes – and Habitat 67 offers a glimpse of what it might be like. Built for Expo 67, the Montreal World's Fair, it was meant to be a model for cities around the world – an attempt to introduce greenery, privacy and other benefits of suburban living to a city apartment building. Its concrete forms are stacked like Lego bricks in multiple combinations up to twelve storeys high. The bricks interlock to form a variety of apartment types, large and small, which open on to landscaped terraces. As an experiment it is both a success and failure – loved by those who live there, but destined to remain a prototype.

Montreal, Canada (1967) Architect: Moshe Safdie

Farmscrapers

Picture a village where you live and work, go to school or to the shops, and where there are fields to grow food. Now imagine that instead of being on the ground, the village is a cross between a farm and a skyscraper – a 'farmscraper'. This cluster of farmscrapers is being built in Shenzhen, in China: one of the most densely populated areas on Earth. The towers are arranged as stacks of 'pebbles', with vegetation on top. The pebbles can contain housing, offices, shops and recreation spaces, depending on need. Each tower is energy self-sufficient and because there is no need to drive anywhere, harmful greenhouse gas emissions are minimised. In the future we might all live and work in farmscrapers.

Shenzhen, China (2013-) Architect: Vincent Callebaut Architectures

Floating cities

Scientists predict that as the Earth warms, sea levels will rise significantly. Low-lying regions may one day vanish beneath the waves. Some coastal communities and small island nations are already suffering the harmful effects of climate change. So where are people to live if their land disappears? Perhaps they will one day live on the water, in floating cities. If these cities could roam the globe, like enormous ocean liners, they need never experience a winter. They could grow their own food under glass. Moored in tidal areas they could harness hydroelectric power. By processing their own waste they could generate natural gas. Floating cities may sound like science fiction, but they are perfectly possible.

World Oceans (2008) Architect: Vincent Callebaut Architectures

Lunar dwelling

The idea of a lunar settlement has fascinated scientists since space exploration began, but building on the Moon has only recently become a possibility, thanks to the latest 3D printing technology. This four-person dwelling starts out as a cylindrical module, transported by space rocket. An inflatable dome unfolds from the module to provide temporary support for a rigid outer shell – a shield against meteorites and other hazards. On Earth this shell would be cast in concrete. Here it is formed from lunar soil, or 'regolith', using a robotic 3D printer. The shell has a cellular structure, similar to ice, which helps to insulate the occupants from lunar temperature fluctuations. Does that sound familiar? It should – it is an igloo on the Moon!

The Moon (2013-) Architects: European Space Agency; Foster + Partners

First published in 2015 by Circa Press
© 2015 Circa Press Limited

Circa Press
50 Great Portland Street
London W1W 7ND
www.circapress.net

ISBN 978-0-9930721-1-6

Cataloguing-in-Publication Data for this book is
available from the British Library

Printed and bound in Italy by Graphicom

Reproduction: Dawkins Colour
Design: Jean-Michel Dentand